Aboriginal Art of Australia

Aboriginal Art of Australia

Exploring Cultural Traditions

BY CAROL FINLEY

LERNER BOOKS ■ LONDON ■ NEW YORK ■ MINNEAPOLIS

For D

This book was first published in the United States of America in 1999.

First published in the United Kingdom in 2008 by
Lerner Books,
Dalton House,
60 Windsor Avenue,
London SW19 2RR

Website address: www.lernerbooks.co.uk

This edition was updated and edited for UK publication by Discovery Books Ltd., Unit 3, 37 Watling Street, Leintwardine, Shropshire SY7 0LW

British Library Cataloguing in Publication Data

Finley, Carol
    Aboriginal art of Australia : exploring cultural
    traditions. - (Art around the world)
    1. Painting, Aboriginal Australian - Juvenile literature
    2. Aboriginal Australians - Juvenile literature
    I. Title
    759.9'94

    ISBN-13: 978 1 58013 372 2

Printed in China

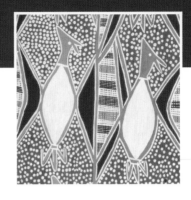

Contents

Introduction
to
Aboriginal Art

A group of Aborigines perform a ceremonial dance.

ABORIGINES ARE THE ORIGINAL PEOPLE OF Australia. They have lived on that continent for 40 thousand years. Living in clans, or groups of related families, the Aborigines were hunters and food gatherers who led a semi-nomadic existence throughout Australia. In addition to the essential duties of obtaining food and building shelters, Aborigines spent their time telling myths, making music, singing songs, dancing and making visual art. A person could only attain a position of authority in this society if he or she had a thorough knowledge of these arts. Isolated from the rest of human-kind for thousands of years, the Aborigines developed their own survival system and a unique belief system. Reverence for the land around them was fundamental to the way each Aboriginal clan lived.

Aboriginal society began to change in 1788, when the British established a permanent settlement at Sydney Cove. The British wanted land for settlements, farms and ranches, so many Aboriginal clans were eventually forced from their ancestral dwelling places.

When the British first arrived in Australia, approximately 300,000 Aborigines were living in 500 to 600 clans. Violent conflict with the new settlers, diseases the settlers carried and a colonial policy that often allowed the Aborigines to be treated cruelly, meant that they suffered extreme hardships and the traditional Aboriginal way of life was irreversibly changed. By 1930, the Aboriginal population had dwindled to 67,000. Some clans had completely died out. The current

(Opposite) The Founding of Australia, painted by Algernon Talmage, shows the unfurling of the British flag at Sydney Cove on 26 January 1788.

Raymond Gamarrawu of the Mirrar Aboriginal people in northern Australia protests against the opening of a second mine on their traditional lands. The Mirrar believe a new mine at nearby Jabiluka could disturb a powerful lizard spirit, resulting in sickness, climate extremes and flooding.

Aboriginal population is about 250,000. They make up 1.5 per cent of the 17.7 million people who live on the Australian continent.

An Aboriginal political movement working for equality and land rights has resulted in some social and economic improvements for the Aboriginal people in Australia. Aborigines were granted citizenship in 1967 and they were given the right to vote in 1984. Recently, many Aborigines have been allowed to claim land that once belonged to their clans and they hold title to about 11 per cent of Australian land. The struggle for social justice continues, however, and remains an important issue.

One way to learn more about the native people of Australia is to study their art. The Aboriginal people have an artistic tradition that dates back thousands of years. Their art included rock paintings and engravings, sand paintings and bark paintings. They also painted designs on objects, such as shields and boomerangs, and did elaborate body painting for dance ceremonies and rituals.

(*Left*) A rock painting in Kakadu National Park in Arnhem Land.

(*Below*) A young Aboriginal boy is being painted for ceremonial dancing.

Painting on canvas and bark is still a flourishing activity in many Aboriginal communities and the work of many artists is internationally acclaimed.

While much of Australia's population is concentrated in the eastern coastal cities, most Aborigines live in remote regions of the continent. This book will look at contemporary paintings from three of these regions: Arnhem Land, the Kimberley and the Desert. Aboriginal painting is unique in both subject matter and style. Styles of art and the materials

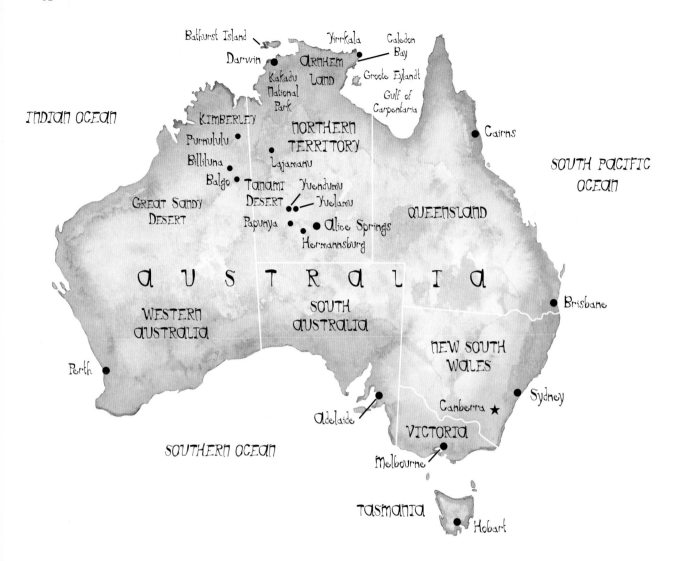

used make it differ from region to region.

Beliefs and traditions vary somewhat from one clan to the next, but one common thread linking Aboriginal people is their view of land. To an Aborigine, land is sacred. The land where their ancestors lived contains their heritage, their history and their spirit.

Much Aboriginal painting is about the land, because it is so valued. Early painting was done directly on the land in the form of rock paintings. Contemporary painting often provides a view of the land or tells a picture story about how features of the landscape were created. Ginger Riley Munduwalawala's *My Country* (**Figure 1**) is an example of a painting that shows the history of the land.

Figure 1. *My Country*, Ginger Riley Munduwalawala, 1988.

Even the shape of the painting resembles the continent of Australia. Munduwalawala's clan, the Mara, lived in Limmen Bight, adjacent to Arnhem Land. Her painting contains birds, snakes, sea creatures and a kangaroo — mythological animals that are important to the painter's clan. Human figures are also portrayed. The person in the right, bottom corner, under a tree, is pointing to a rectangular box. This box is called a 'message stick'. The painter uses it to announce a ceremony or rite, or to invite the viewer to visit his or her homeland. A larger message stick, flanked by two snakes, appears in the left bottom section of the painting.

Can you understand the Aborigines' strong attachment to their homeland? Can you think of a place that you would like to celebrate in a song or painting?

The Dreaming

Aboriginal paintings are not primarily decorative objects. They have a deeper meaning associated with Aboriginal myths and beliefs. One concept that is central to Aboriginal belief systems is called Dreaming, or Dreamtime. To understand the paintings, viewers must understand this concept.

To Aborigines, the word 'Dreamtime' does not refer to an individual's imaginings during sleep. The term refers to the Aboriginal understanding of how the land and its people were created. The Dreamtime could be described as a set of Aboriginal religious beliefs concerning creation.

A 300 million-year-old sandstone outcrop in the Kimberley region of north-western Australia.

An Aboriginal burial ground.

According to Aboriginal beliefs, supernatural beings with magical powers inhabited the Earth before human history began. The Earth had been a flat, barren surface until these beings sculpted it, creating all the features of the landscape by taking the shapes of snakes, kangaroos, lizards, emus, dingoes, grubs and other creatures. Mountains, plateaus, rivers and valleys were all believed to have been made during the Dreamtime.

The Dreamtime also explains how natural forces, such as thunder and rain, and living things, such as plants, animals and people, came into existence. Part of Dreamtime's uniqueness is its connection to the land.

Not only are the myths part of the Aborigines' oral history, passed down from generation to generation, but evidence of the Dreamtime account is believed to be recorded in the features of the landscape that the Aborigines can see around them. For example, a particular mountain ridge may have been made during the kangaroo Dreaming. The mythological activities of this creature could also be told in a story or by making a painting.

Different myths are important to different clans and different features of the landscape illustrate these myths. Aboriginal artists choose their subjects from among their own clan's myths and paint only the myths that are associated with their own clan. To paint a particular Dreaming demonstrates hereditary ownership of it and the land associated with it. It is not considered ethical or even legal to paint the Dreamings that belong to another clan.

The landscape itself can be viewed as a giant book in which the ancient mythological history of the Aborigines is recorded. The Aborigines have had disputes with the Australian government regarding construction projects — such as roads — that would change the look of the landscape because they believe their land is sacred, and the powers and the spirits of their ancestors lie within it. Aborigines sometimes go on 'Walkabout', which is a pilgrimage that might last for weeks at a time. During a Walkabout, Aborigines walk across the land, visiting the important Dreaming sites of their clan. Sometimes they sing songs that have been passed down along with the myths. The lyrics of these songs may describe the landscape and tell about the Dreamtime creatures that brought it into being.

Painting is one way the Aborigines convey their beliefs to others. While you may never see the features of the Australian landscape or go on a Walkabout, you can look at Aboriginal paintings to gain an understanding of their culture and beliefs.

chapter one

The Bark Paintings of Arnhem Land

A paperbark swamp at Mabaloodoo Escarpment in western Arnhem Land.

(Opposite and above) Bark must be carefully removed from the tree and allowed to dry before it is ready for painting.

ARNHEM LAND AND ITS SURROUNDING ISLANDS in Australia's Northern Territory are rich in environmental diversity. Rock plateaus, jungles and forests exist in this region, where the traditional Aboriginal lifestyle still flourishes. Once a reserve for Aboriginal people, similar to Native American reservations in the United States, much of the area is now under the jurisdiction of the Aborigines themselves.

The art tradition in this area is old and distinctive. Rock painting, which dates back tens of thousands of years, is still practised. In recent times, the area is best known for bark painting, a traditional Aboriginal art form that is hundreds of years old. Within the Arnhem Land, regional stylistic differences in bark painting exist, but the technique of painting on bark is similar throughout the area.

Artists use natural materials from the environment for painting. They peel large sections of bark off eucalyptus trees and let them dry. Then they remove the textured outer layer of bark and use the smooth interior layer as the 'canvas'. Aboriginal painters traditionally use red, yellow, white and black paints. They are made from mined ochre, clay and charcoal. Brushes can be made from hair, plant fibre, feathers or twigs.

The artist chooses a subject for the painting from the myths, animal stories and designs that belong to the clan. To understand the intention of the artist and the full meaning of the painting would require a knowledge of Aboriginal myth, ceremony and beliefs held only by clan elders. Outsiders can only relate to the art as deeply as they understand the people and myths expressed in it. You can partially learn the meaning of the art, however, by becoming acquainted with Aboriginal beliefs and developing an appreciation for their artistic creations. In this way, paintings from the Arnhem Land give you a window into another world.

The Mimi Myth

Until recently, the Aboriginal culture did not have a written language. Stories, legends and myths have been passed down by storytellers from generation to generation. The stories are recorded as paintings, which can take the place of a book. The Mimi myth, for example, is a popular subject for bark painting.

Mimis were very thin, mischievous spirit beings who lived in rocks and caves. They were so thin that they had to avoid being blown by wind, which might break their necks or carry them away. The Mimis helped the early Aborigines learn to hunt and also to paint. In some legends, Mimis would lure people into caves and hold them captive.

Ancient rock paintings of Mimi figures exist in caves in the Arnhem Land. The belief in Mimis is very old, as is the tradition of painting these beings. *Mimi Spirits* **(Figure 2)** by Yirawala was painted around 1970. It

Ancient rock paintings of Mimi figures can be seen on the walls of many caves.

shows three adult Mimis and four children. These tall figures have small heads, gaping mouths, long necks and especially long arms. Their hair is a series of fine parallel lines. The Mimi on the far right is a male figure who has feathers growing out of his knees and ankles. The Mimis to his left are female figures. The bodies of the large Mimis have

Figure 2.
Mimi Spirits,
Yirawala,
circa 1970.

Figure 3.
The Constellation of Scorpio, Larrtjunga, 1959.

been partially coloured in with a geometric pattern. Sometimes such patterns in paintings are associated with a particular clan. Yirawala has chosen the traditional colours — red, yellow and white.

The Stars

People throughout the world have looked up into the sky and imagined figures and stories. The constellations are also a subject of Arnhem Land artists. *The Constellation of Scorpio* (Figure 3) by Larrtjunga, from north-eastern Arnhem Land, shows three bright stars at the top of the painting. Towards the centre of the picture, three spirits sit around a fire, one playing a *didjeridoo*, a musical instrument made from the hollowed-out branch of a tree. A large crocodile with a series of stars on it appears on the right. A small opossum stands beside it and two ibis (wading birds) are on the left side of the painting. Perhaps this painting is a scene the artist imagined when he looked at the constellation of Scorpio.

Figure 4. *Orion and the Pleiades,* Minimini Mamarika, 1948.

Orion and the Pleiades (**Figure 4**) by Minimini Mamarika is another constellation painting. Mamarika is from Groote Eyelandt, which is an island 48 kilometres off the coast of Arnhem Land. Bark paintings from this area are often painted on a black background. The T-shape represents Orion's Belt and the horizontal stars represent three fishermen. Four stars in the vertical row represent three fish caught by the men and the fire over which they cooked the fish. Above the T-shape is a circular shape depicting the Pleiades. In one myth, this is said to represent a grass hut. Inside are the stars that represent the wives of the fishermen, called *burumburumrunya.*

Animals in Painting

Animals found on the Australian continent are widespread in Aboriginal art and mythology. Some of the animals are not found anywhere else in the world. Kangaroos, wallabies, bandicoots, goa lizards, birds and fish are among those often portrayed. Aboriginal artists, however, paint animals in the context of their activities during the Dreamtime, when the features of the land were being formed. Certain Aboriginal clans believe they are descended from particular Dreamtime animals that are considered sacred.

Short-nosed Bandicoot

Kangaroo

Koala Bear

Emu

Wallaby

Figure 5.
Wongarr Dog of the
Ganalbingu Clan,
Tony Djikululu,
1979.

Figure 6. *Fight between Mildal, the Blue-Tongued Lizard and Dadbagururumulu, the King Brown Snake,* Paddy Fordham Wainburranga, 1984.

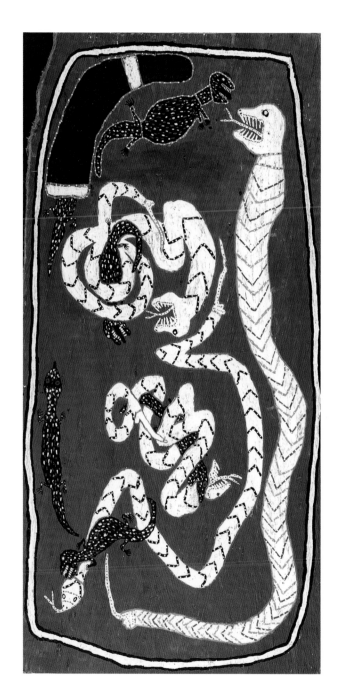

Wongarr Dog of the Ganalbingu Clan (**Figure 5**) by Tony Djikululu illustrates a Dreamtime episode. A Dreamtime being and his dog were travelling through the Arnhem Land. During their journey they entered a cave where they found a colony of flying foxes nesting. This painting shows a group of the flying foxes in the cave.

Snakes are a favourite subject for Australian Aboriginal painters throughout the continent. Paddy Fordham Wainburranga's painting *Fight between Mildal, the Blue-Tongued Lizard and Dadbagururumulu, the King Brown Snake* (**Figure 6**) shows several scenes of a snake and a lizard fighting. They both look ferocious, displaying their sharp teeth. The fight ends with the lizard running into a hollow log to escape the snake. This is shown in the upper left corner of the painting. Can you read the scenes in this painting?

Figure 7. *Untitled*, Unknown Artist
from Yirrkala, undated.

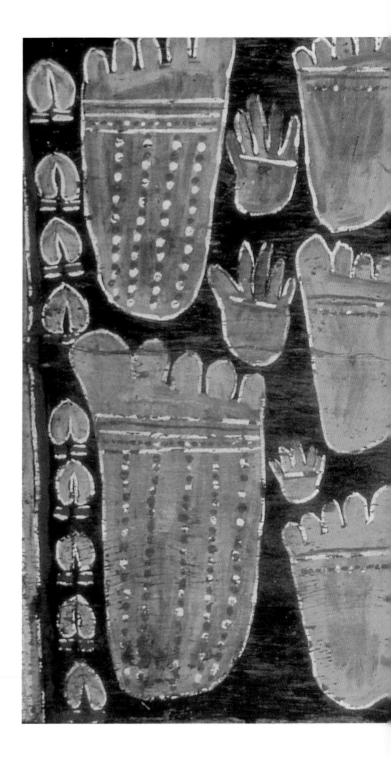

Tracks and Footprints

The Aborigines were skilled hunters and their
ability to observe, identify and follow the
tracks of animals was of crucial importance.
In Aboriginal paintings, the tracks of animals
and the footprints of humans are often depicted. In fact, sometimes just the footprints
or tracks will be painted to represent an animal or a person. In this bark painting **(Figure
7)** by an unknown artist from Yirrkala in
north-eastern Arnhem Land, there are human
footprints and handprints of various sizes. A
larger footprint might represent a more important person. A whole series of footprints,
such as those in this painting, might suggest a
journey taken. On the far left of the bark
there is a vertical row of kidney-shaped forms.
These are stingray livers, a dish considered a
delicacy in that region.

Aboriginal artists from other regions of Australia paint subjects similar to those that appear in Arnhem Land works, but other artists use different materials and paint in different styles.

An Aboriginal man hunting near Ramingining in Arnhem Land.

chapter two

The Kimberley
Region

Chamberlain Gorge in eastern Kimberley.

Broad-trunked baobab trees grow in western Kimberley.

KIMBERLEY IS THE NAME OF A REGION WEST of Arnhem Land. Many Aboriginal clans live in this area. Kimberley artists often use naturally occurring pigments, similar to paints used by the Arnhem Land artists. They also use synthetic, commercially manufactured, acrylic paints, as the desert artists do. Artists of the Kimberley usually paint on composition board or canvas.

Wandjina

Kimberley is famous for paintings of *Wandjina* — both in old paintings on rocks and in contemporary works of art. Wandjina are mythological beings said to have come out of the sky and sea during an ancient time. When their time on Earth was finished, they are believed to have left their images — in the form of paintings — on the surfaces of rocks. Wandjina are portrayed as human-like beings. They are usually depicted in black, red or yellow over a white background, and halos or strands of hair radiate from their heads. Their spirits are still believed to inhabit the places where their images are found.

Ignatia Jangarra's painting *Wandjina* (**Figure 8**) on page 35 shows two Wandjina looking out from the canvas. The Wandjina have eyes with prominently painted eyelashes, noses represented by vertical lines, but no mouths. Strands of hair jut out from their heads. The heads, necks and shoulders of the figures are a ghostly white. They are wearing a costume that has a

Figure 8.
Wandjina,
Ignatia Jangarra,
1992.

reddish brown pattern painted on white and a black semicircular shape at mid-chest level. This way of depicting the neck and shoulders and the shape shown on the middle chest is typical of Wandjina paintings. The background of the painting is made up of black dots. A large, black snake stretches above the head of one Wandjina and below the left hand of the other. Snakes are often associated with Wandjina in stories. On the right side of the painting there are also two emus and a lizard painted in reddish brown outline.

It is believed that Wandjina shaped the characteristics of the landscape and were the ancestors of some present-day Aborigines in the Kimberley area. The Wandjina were thought to have the power to control certain forces of nature, such as rain, lightning and cyclones. They also influenced fertility.

Wandjina could, if they were angry, kill people with heavy rains, floods or lightning. They could also bring good luck in hunting, fishing and food gathering if they wanted to be helpful. Ceremonies with special songs were conducted by Aborigines to communicate with the Wandjina and ask for the good fortune they could bring. Few Aborigines still believe in the Wandjina myth, but the Wandjina remains an enduring image in Aboriginal art.

Figure 9. *Wandjina*, Alec Mingelmanganu, 1980.

Alec Mingelmanganu's 1980 painting *Wandjina* **(Figure 9)** shows a large, powerful-looking Wandjina that fills most of the canvas. This imposing figure conveys the Wandjina's immense strength to the viewer.

Weather

Weather is a frequent subject in Aboriginal art. For traditional Aborigines who lived in a harsh environment without permanent shelters, the weather conditions would be of utmost importance and severe weather would

sometimes be a matter of life and death. In paintings, mythological storms and floods from the Dreamtime are portrayed in addition to recent weather events.

On Christmas Day in 1974, a major cyclone hit Darwin, a city in Arnhem Land and the largest city in northern Australia. This disastrous event caused extensive damage. Some Aborigines interpreted the cyclone as a warning from Dreamtime ancestors about contemporary life. Rover Thomas, a well-known Kimberley artist from Warmun, did a series of paintings about this event. *Cyclone*

Aborigines camping at Caledon Bay in the Northern Territory.

Figure 10. *Cyclone Tracy*, Rover Thomas, 1991.

Figure 11. *Dreamtime Story of the Willy Willy,* Rover Thomas, 1989.

Tracy **(Figure 10)**, done in 1991, is one of these paintings. The large black mass is the cyclone. The smaller shapes branching off from the cyclone represent smaller wind forces caused by the cyclone.

Rover Thomas also painted *Dreamtime Story of the Willy Willy* **(Figure 11)**. The Willy Willy is the name used for a spiralling dust storm that can occur in desert areas. Here, the artist shows the path of the storm as it

winds around to its final destination – a water hole shown at the centre of the painting.

Can you think of a weather event that you witnessed and would like to use as the subject of a work of art?

Christianity

Some Aborigines have converted to Christianity and have taken stories from the Bible as a new source of subject matter. In *God Sending the Holy Spirit* (**Figure 12**), the artist Queenie McKenzie has painted the Pentecost,

The Bathurst Island Mission Catholic Church, with a decorated altar and a tabernacle of ironwood inlaid with shells.

Figure 12.
God Sending the Holy Spirit,
Queenie McKenzie,
1991.

a Christian feast day that falls 50 days after Easter and commemorates the gift of the Holy Spirit being sent to the church. In the painting, Jesus is the large figure bestowing the Holy Spirit on the apostles. The Holy Spirit emanates as white light from the body of Jesus. A painting like this is a reminder that art is an ever-changing tradition. Like other artists, Aboriginal artists are exposed to new ideas and new doctrines. As the world around them changes, artists adopt new subject matter or paint traditional subjects in new ways.

chapter three

The Desert
Paintings

(Left) A scene from the Tanami Desert, near Balgo.

(Below) A large, desert sand painting made of coloured gravel by members of the Ipolera Aboriginal community, near Hermannsburg in the Northern Territory.

CONTEMPORARY PAINTING IS FLOURISHING IN the desert area, from Alice Springs to the western coast of Australia. Aboriginal people from the desert have a tradition of body painting, painting on objects such as boomerangs and water carriers and making elaborate ground sculptures from sand, feathers, clay, sticks and other natural materials. The contemporary painting movement of the desert areas presents works that are brilliantly coloured and rich in mythological symbols.

Contemporary desert painting began its development in 1971 when Geoff Bardon, a teacher in Papunya, encouraged children and adults to paint murals. Out of this project grew a great interest in painting. Bardon brought materials such as canvasses and acrylic paints into the Aboriginal community, and a renewed interest in art emerged.

The Australian government had built the Papunya settlement in the 1950s to relocate Aborigines from several clans. Aboriginal people who had lost free access to their ancestral lands due to infringing cattle and mining interests were often moved to settlements away from their homelands during the 1950s and 1960s. The government settlement at Papunya was a dismal failure, but somehow out of the despair of the Aborigines who lived there, a brilliant art form developed. Contemporary painting became a source of pride, as well as a way of making a living for desert artists.

Painting on canvas later spread to other areas of the desert, notably Yuendumu, Lajamanu and Balgo. Using acrylic paint,

Cassidy Ulluru is telling the story of the battle between Liru (Brown Snake Man) and Kuniya (Python Man).

Aboriginal artists incorporated traditional motifs and Dreamtime symbols that belonged to their clan. Sometimes several Dreamings would be incorporated into a single painting. It is not uncommon for many artists to work on one painting, particularly on the larger canvases that might measure a metre or more across.

Acrylic paintings from the desert have been exhibited at museums and galleries around the world. Painting a series of dots is the prevalent technique of the desert artists. The dots give the paintings a mosaic quality. Some paintings are made entirely of dots, while in others, dots make certain forms. Western Desert artists often paint a series of lines and circles. At first glance, some of the desert paintings look like abstract art — art without a recognizable subject. The viewer needs certain information to understand these paintings better. For example, concentric circles may depict a campfire and U shapes may depict people sitting around a campfire. The paintings tell an Aboriginal story in the same way that dance, myth or song would. To the outsider, the desert paintings may be the most difficult to interpret, but viewers can learn something about the subject matter by consulting Dreamtime myths.

Figure 13.
Bandicoot Dreaming,
Mick Namarari
Tjapaltjarri, 1991.

Animal Tracks

Bandicoot Dreaming (**Figure 13**) by Mick Namarari Tjapaltjarri shows a circle with a band around it in the centre of the painting. Straight and curved lines radiate from the circle, which represents a hole the bandicoot dug in the sand. The lines represent the marks the bandicoot made in the sand when it dug the hole. In a legend, the bandicoot —

Figure 14. *Yankirri Jukurrpa [Emu Dreaming]*, Darby Jampijinpa Ross, 1987.

a small, ratlike mammal found in Australia — got its spots during an argument with the moon. When the moon threw a handful of dry clay at the bandicoot, the clay stuck to its body, giving the bandicoot spots. The artist who made this painting chose not to paint a bandicoot directly, but to represent the animal by painting its tracks. Can you imagine the lines in this painting to be the bandicoot's tracks left after he dug a hole?

Dreamtime

Emus are large, Australian birds that can run fast but cannot fly. They stand about one and a half metres tall and weigh about 45 kilograms. Their small wings are hidden in their feathers. Emus are important mythological Dreamtime beings for some Aboriginal clans. *Yankirri Jukurrpa [Emu Dreaming]* (**Figure 14**) is a painting by Darby Jampijinpa Ross, an artist from Yuendumu. In the painting, emus are represented by rows of arrowlike tracks radiating out from just beyond the centre of the painting. In the centre is a circular form that represents a water hole. The emus are making their way to the water hole. Shapes representing digging sticks or spears appear between the rows of emu tracks. The long squiggly lines represent the intestines of the emus. Ross painted the tracks, intestines, spears and sticks a dark colour. The background of these

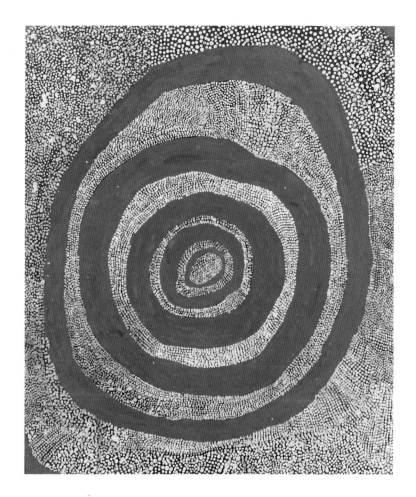

Figure 15.
Snake and Water Dreaming,
Yala Yala Tjungurrayi, 1972.

images, which is supposed to show the land, is painted in a brilliant display of red, yellow, green and white. The painting, which depicts the mythical travels of the emus' Dreamtime ancestors, is alive with a vibrant sense of colour and movement.

The snake is also an important mythological animal for the Aborigines and it appears in many of their paintings. As a Dreamtime ancestor for some clans, the snake instructed people to be kind to one another. In some areas, snakes were thought to be responsible for controlling rains — something of crucial importance for people living off the land in the desert. *Snake and Water Dreaming* (**Figure 15**) is by Yala Yala Tjungurrayi, one of the early painters who worked at Papunya and one of the leaders of his clan. This painting, done entirely in reddish brown earth tones, white and black, shows a snake coiled up in its water hole or home. The snake is painted in reddish brown concentric circles. The white dots that make up the background of the painting represent the snake's eggs.

The painting can also represent the place where the mythological snake broke through the Earth's surface during the Dreamtime.

Uta Uta Tjangala was another one of the early group of painters working at Papunya. Some of his work was done on a large scale and involved other painters from his community. The subjects that Uta Uta Tjangala chose were the important Dreamtime sites and beings associated with his clan. One of these is *Yumari* **(Figure 16),** a sacred place in the desert with secret water sources. In this painting the water holes are shown as colourful concentric circles. The Yumari site plays an important role in Aboriginal mythology. It is a place where secret ceremonies for those belonging to the clan would take place. Uta Uta Tjangala was one of the leaders of his clan and had special responsibilities regarding the Yumari site.

Figure 16. *Yumari,* Uta Uta Tjangala, undated.

An Aboriginal artist at work in a gallery in Alice Springs.

Conclusion

(Opposite) Two Aboriginal women on a gathering expedition.

ABORIGINAL ARTISTS BRING VIEWERS INTO THEIR world through their art. The stories their paintings tell are unique to their culture and not always easily accessible to outsiders. Their paintings are splendid works of art which offer us a glimpse into Aboriginal society and their feelings about the land and the life it supports. On the pages of this book you have been introduced to flying foxes, snakes and bandicoots. Through their work, Aboriginal artists have conveyed their feelings about the importance of safeguarding the land — an important message for everyone in the world to hear.

For Further Reading

Bancroft, Bronwyn. *Patterns of Australia* Little Hare, 2006.

Bingham, Jane. *Aboriginal Art & Culture* (World Art & Culture) Raintree, 2006.

Cahir, Sandra. *Livewire Investigates Aboriginal Studies Arts and Symbols* (Livewires) Cambridge University Press, 2002

Selected Bibliography

Allen, Louis A. *Time before Morning.* New York: Thomas Y. Crowell Company, 1975.

Berndt, Ronald M. and Catherine H. Berndt. *The Speaking Land.* Rochester, Vt: Inner Traditions International, 1994.

Caruana, Wally. *Aboriginal Art.* New York: Thames and Hudson, 1994.

Isaacs, Jennifer. *Australian Aboriginal Paintings.* New York: Dutton Studio Books, 1989.

Mudrooroo Nyoongah. *Aboriginal Mythology.* London: Thorsons, 1994.

Ryan, Judith. *Images of Power: Aboriginal Art of the Kimberley.* Melbourne: National Gallery of Victoria, 1993.

——. *Mythscapes: Aboriginal Art of the Desert.* Melbourne: National Gallery of Victoria, 1989.

Sutton, Peter, ed. *Dreamings: The Art of Aboriginal Australia.* New York: The Asia Society Galleries and George Braziller, Inc., 1988.

Index

About the Author

Carol Finley studied art history at Northwestern University, USA, and did graduate work at Bryn Mawr College, Philadelphia, USA. She worked as a trader in the financial markets before pursuing a career in writing. She lives in London and New York City.

Photo Acknowledgements

The Alcaston Gallery, Melbourne, Australia, (Courtesy of the estate of the artist and Alcaston Gallery, Melbourne), back cover, 7 [detail], 13; © Louis A. Allen, 18 (top and bottom right), 20, 23; AP Photo/Wide World Photos/Sandy Scheltema, 10; Art Gallery of South Australia, Adelaide, (Minimini Mamarika, Australia, 1904-1972, Orion and the Pleiades, 1948, Umbakumba, Groote Eylandt, Northern Territory, natural pigments on eucalyptus bark 77.0 x 32.5 cm (irreg), South Australian Government Grant 1957, Art Gallery of South Australia, Adelaide), 24; Australian Museum/Nature Focus, Sydney, 28-29; © Bill Bachman, 11 (bottom), 14, 18 (left), 32 (left), 32-33, 41, 44 (both), 46; © Michele Burgess, 25 (centre middle); © Bettmann/CORBIS, 8 (bottom); © Mark Hakansson/Panos Pictures, 52 (top); © Images International/Erwin C. 'Bud' Nielsen, 25 (left); © Buddy Mays/TRAVEL STOCK, 25 (right); Museum and Art Gallery of the Northern Territory, (Wongarr Dog of the Ganalbingu Clan, ABART-0661) © DACS London, 2007, 5 [detail], 26, (Bandicoot Dreaming, WAL-0268), 47; National Gallery of Australia, Canberra, (Cyclone Tracy), 2, 38, (Fight Between Mildal, the Blue-Tongued Lizard and Dadbagururumulu, the King Brown Snake, Founding Donor Fund 1984) © DACS London, 2007, 27; National Gallery of Victoria, Melbourne, Australia, (Wandjina, by A. Mingelmanganu, Purchased from Admissions Funds, 1990), front cover, 31 [detail], 36, (Wandjina by Ignatia Jangarra, Private Collection), 35, (Dreamtime Story of the Willy Willy, Felton Bequest, 1990), 39, (God Sending the Holy Spirit, Purchased through the Art Foundation of Victoria, with the assistance of the Alcoa Foundation, Governor, 1991), 40, (Yankirri Jukurrpa—Emu Dreaming, Purchased through the Art Foundation of Victoria with the assistance of Lauraine Diggins, Fellow, 1987) © DACS London, 2007, 43 [detail], 49, (Snake and Water Dreaming, Gift of Mrs. D. Carnegie OAM, 1989), 50; Office of Public Affairs, Australian Embassy, Washington D.C., 25 (centre top and centre bottom); © Kay Shaw, 11 (top), 15; South Australian Museum, Photographer: M. Kluvanek (Mimi Spirits, Sandra Le Brun Holmes collection), 17 [detail], 21; Jennifer Steele/Art Resource, NY, (© Aboriginal Artists Agency Limited. Collection Robert Holmes a Court, Perth, Australia), 51; © SuperStock, Inc, 8 (top), 19, 37; © Penny Tweedie/Panos Pictures, 30, 52 (bottom); Laura Westlund, 12.

Lerner Books gratefully acknowledges the following individuals/agencies for their assistance in obtaining permission to reproduce the artwork that appears in this book:

Anthony Wallis and the Aboriginal Artists Agency Limited on behalf of:
Mick Namarari Tjapaltjarri (Bandicoot Dreaming)
Minimini Mamarika (Orion and the Pleiades)
Yala Yala Tjungurrayi (Snake and Water Dreaming)
Uta Uta Tjangala (Yumari)
Alec Mingelmanganu (Wandjina)
Yirawala (Mimi Spirits)

Mary Macha and Aboriginal Arts and Crafts on behalf of:
Ignatia Jangarra (Wandjina)

Beverly Knight and the Alcaston Gallery on behalf of:
Ginger Riley Munduwalawala (My Country)

Warmun Art Centre and Jane Yalunga on behalf of:
Rover Thomas (Cyclone Tracy, Dreamtime Story of the Willy Willy)

Andrew Blake and Buku-Larrnggay Mulka Centre on behalf of the Ganambarr family and the Yolngu of Yirrkala, on behalf of:
Larrtjunga (The Constellation of Scorpio)
Artist from Yirrkala (Untitled)

Kevin Kelly on behalf of:
Queenie McKenzie (God Sending the Holy Spirit)

Viscopy/DACS on behalf of:
Darby Jampijinpa Ross (Yankirri Jukurrpa—Emu Dreaming)
Paddy Fordham Wainburranga (Fight Between Mildal. . . . and Dadbagurururmulu)
Tony Djikululu (Wongarr Dog of the Ganalbingu Clan)